For Mark

Jane Seabrook

With text by Ashleigh Brilliant

Furry Logic

LOVE

Ten Speed Press

Berkeley

I'm on the brink of happiness—

will you give me a push?

My interest in you

at present is

somewhere between

hopeless love and

idle curiosity.

Are we having a relationship, or just doing resear

n each other?

Your love may be as close as I will ever

get to heaven.

I'm utterly

dazzled by your inner beauty.

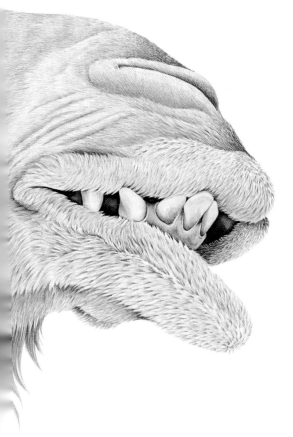

I'm sure I could make you happy,

if only you'd

lower your

standards

drastically.

Come out of your shell

into mine.

I

don't know

whether to

run away

with you or

from you.

You are not perfect—

but some of your

imperfections

are

strangely attractive.

I have you

you have me

at least one of us is lucky.

Am I t

Or n

As long as I have you, there's just one

other thing I'll always need —

tremendous self-control.

The secret of being a good lover is …

not knowing when to stop.

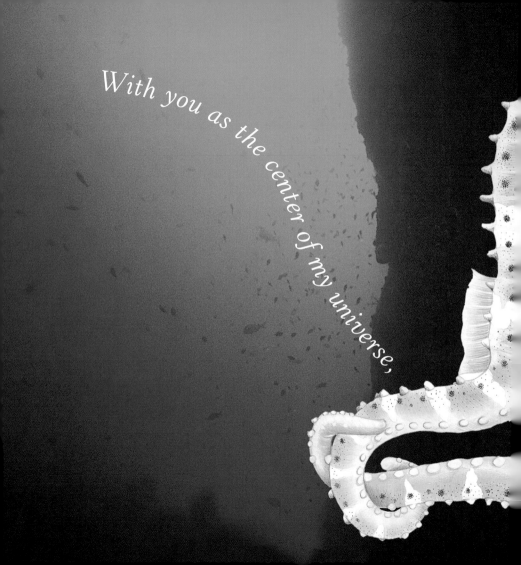

With you as the center of my universe,

no wonder my orbit is so erratic.

Anyone can be passionate...

but it takes real lovers to be silly.

How would you rate me, on a scale of

wonderful to *marvelous?*

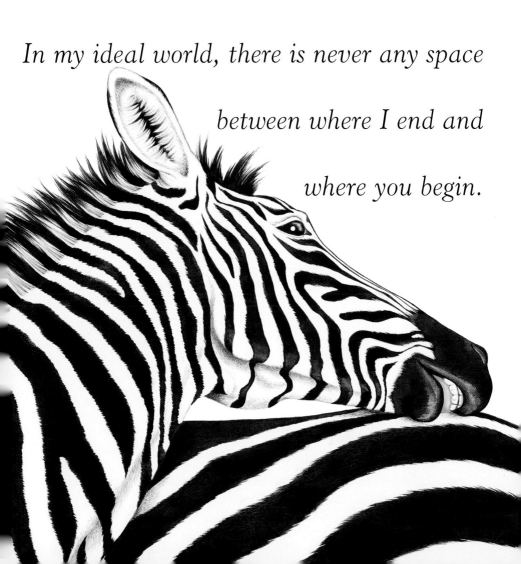

In my ideal world, there is never any space

between where I end and

where you begin.

Caution: you are in danger of becoming

essential to my way of life.

Try to say it in the fewest possible words,

unless you're saying that you love me.

Don't interrupt me while I'm

giving you my undivided attention.

I wish relationships

could be tested in advance

for safety, comfort, and durability.

I want you, happiness, and chocolate,

but not necessarily in that order.

You've told me you love me,

but there's no harm in

repeating it endlessly.

On second thought,

words are not enough! Send me

candy.

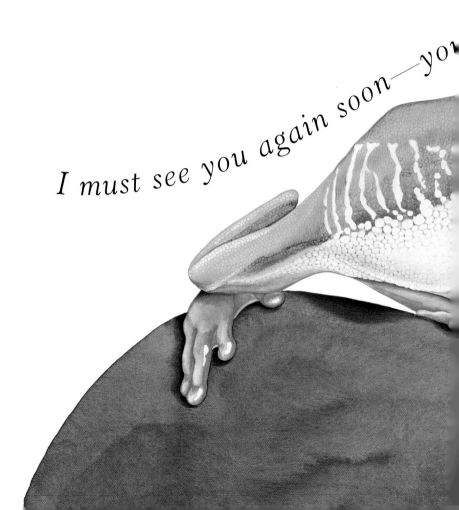

I must see you again soon—you

ffects are beginning to wear off.

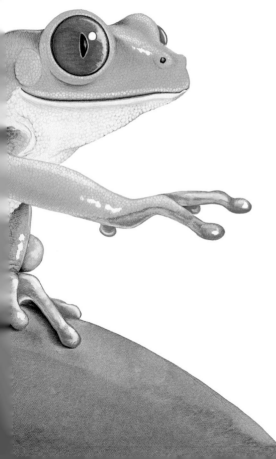

Artist's Notes

Today is Valentine's Day, February 14, 2010, and I am working away on this book of love, the one you are now holding, for the next Valentine's Day in 2011. It will be a gift from me to my valentine. The contents of the book, the book you've just read, will be a surprise for him. He hasn't been allowed to see any of it and keeping it under wraps hasn't been easy. Usually, we are quite a team—I ask his advice and he's careful to tell me what I want to hear. It's a routine that has worked very well for all my previous books. But this time the book has been kept a secret from him. He knows I'm working on it, but that's about all, and unless the date has now passed February 14, 2011, it is still under wraps. On that date, we'll go somewhere nice for dinner, and I will bring out this book at some opportune moment, maybe over dessert, and he'll see the illustrations and all of it for the first time. He'd better like it—or else!

The artist on her wedding day,
May 1, 1979

We were married, my valentine and I, thirty-one years ago on May Day, 1979. But in terms of longevity we are amateurs when it comes to the truly long-married. Herbert and Zelmyra Fisher from North Carolina have celebrated eighty-five remarkable years of marriage together and recently shared their secrets for a happy marriage with the world on Twitter. Their recipe is simple: be great friends, be a team, be supportive, and "love each other with ALL of your heart." Just a few little things to keep in mind each and every day.

Best wishes,

Jane.

For more information, including how to purchase any of the original paintings that appear in this book, visit www.furrylogicbooks.com.

Love is a place where

you always feel at home.

Furry Logic Who's Who

Because I'm sometimes asked to identify the animals, birds, and insects I've painted, I've named them here—from the familiar and recognizable to the more unusual among them such as the ferocious-looking stag beetle, the delicate and tiny New Zealand rifleman, and the shining cuckoo, another native of New Zealand. In order of appearance they are:

1.

20.

19.

2.

3.

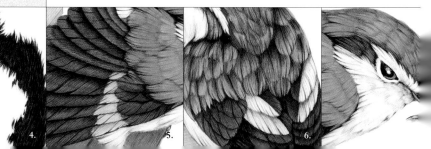

4.

5.

6.

1. Magellanic penguin 2. Rockhopper penguin

3. Crowned crane 4. Magellanic penguin

5. Male New Zealand rifleman 6. Female rifleman

7. Love offering 8. White's tree frog

9. Camel 10. Hermit crab 11. Lesser flamingo

12. Male magnificent frigate bird

13. Female magnificent frigate bird 14. Green tree frog

15. Impala antelope 16. Blue and yellow macaw 17. Lion

18. Seahorse 19. Butterfly

20. Atlantic puffin

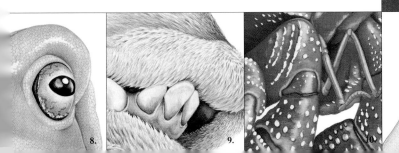

Furry Logic Who's Who

21. Grevy's zebra 22. Erect-crested penguin
23. Yellow-crowned parakeet 24. Siberian tiger
25. Stag beetle 26. Toco toucan
27. Eastern rosella 28. Pig 29. Red-eyed tree frog
30. Chipmunk 31. Shining cuckoo

Jane Seabrook is an illustrator and designer who works from home in her country studio on the outskirts of Auckland, New Zealand. She shares her life with her husband, two adult children, and three utterly adorable Birman cats.

For more information, including how to purchase any of the original paintings that appear in this book, visit www.furrylogicbooks.com.

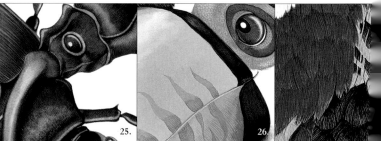

Other Books by Jane Seabrook

Furry Logic: A Guide to Life's Little Challenges

Furry Logic Parenthood

Furry Logic Laugh at Life

The Pick of Furry Logic

Furry Logic Wild Wisdom

Purry Logic

Furry Logic Don't Worry!

Acknowledgments

With the exception of *Anyone can be passionate... but it takes real lovers to be silly.* (Rose Franken) all quotations are by Ashleigh Brilliant. Grateful thanks to Ashleigh, whose Pot-Shot series of epigrams provided most of the words for this book.

For more information, including thousands more of Ashleigh Brilliant's Pot-Shots, visit www.ashleighbrilliant.com.

Thank you!

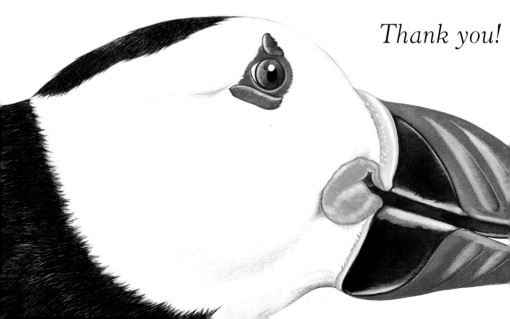

Thank you to everyone at Ten Speed Press for all their support and encouragement, especially my editor, Lisa Westmoreland.

A big thank you to Troy Caltaux and Alex Trimbach, Image Centre, New Zealand.

Text appearing on page 32 from *Another Claudia* by Rose Franken (originally published by
Farrar & Rinehart, Inc., New York, 1943).
All other text by Ashleigh Brilliant. Used by permission.
Photograph on pages 30–31 used by permission of Image Centre Ltd.

Library of Congress Cataloging-in-Publication Data
Seabrook, Jane.
Furry logic love / by Jane Seabrook. -- 1st ed.
p. cm.
Summary: "Artist Jane Seabrook presents a new menagerie of sweet and
snarky animals who have a lot to say about love and relationships"
—Provided by publisher.
1. Conduct of life—Humor. 2. Animals—Pictorial works. I. Title.
PN6231.C6142S428 2010
818'.602—dc22

2010009030

ISBN 978-1-58008-817-6

Printed in China

10 9 8 7 6 5 4 3 2 1

First Edition